www.DiosdadoXi.com

I0115955

www.DiosdadoXi.com
The Bizarro State

Reinaldo Aguiar, a former Google Search engineer
2025 Version 2.1.1

Copyright Notice

For Sebastian and Marcelo.

REINALDO AGUIAR

Never yield to force; never yield to the apparently overwhelming
might of the enemy.
-—Winston Churchill
Speech at Harrow School, October 29, 1941

Table of Contents

Copyright Notice 4
Table of Contents 8
Volume II: www.DiosdadoXi.com: The Bizarro State 9

Prologue: The Jogger and the Index 9
Introduction: A Journey into the Bizarro State 10
Part 1: The Architects - The Rise of the Founding Fathers 12
Chapter 1: The Counter-Intelligence Engine 13
Chapter 2: The Doctrine of Immunity 14
Chapter 3: The Unholy Trinity 15
Part 2: The Global Machine - Anatomy of a Shadow Government 17
Chapter 1: The Paramilitary Force 18
Chapter 2: The Presidents' Club 18
Chapter 3: The Outcasts List 19
Chapter 3: The Global Bureaucracy 20
Chapter 4: The Siege of Windsor Castle 22
Chapter 5: The Infiltration of the Deep State 23
Chapter 6: The Midland Hub - Anatomy of a Micro-Lever 25
Chapter 7: The Election Machine 27
Chapter 8: The Bizarro State's Playbook 28
Tactic 7: Control the Children's Schools 34
Tactic 8: Control the Supply Chain 35
Tactic 10: The Ubiquitous Ledger 36
Chapter 9: The Moscow Center of Gravity 39

5

Chapter 11: The Captive Nations Model 40
Chapter 11: The Cultural Front** 44
Chapter 12: The 3% Racket 45
The 6% Racket 48
An Investigative Blueprint 49
Chapter 15: The Energy Drink Monopoly 51
Chapter 17: The Intelligence Aggregators 52
Part 3: The War for Reality - Scripting the 21st Century 53
Chapter 1: The Propaganda Machine 54
Chapter 2: Turning East: The Battle for Gaza 56
**Chapter 3: Chapter 3: The Economic War 56
**Chapter 4: The Bio-Economic War - A Modern Balkanization 58
Chapter 5: The Nuclear Gambit 60
An Interlude: The Peace Maker 61
Part 4: The Philosophy of the Bizarro State 63
Chapter 1: The Union Theory 64
Chapter 2: The Taxonomy of Predators 65
Chapter 3: The Stanford Prison Experiment, at Scale 65
Chapter 4: The 2% Attack - Hollowing Out Society from Within 66
Chapter 5: The Self-Reinforcing Cycle 68
Chapter 6: The Nuclear Gambit 69
Chapter 7: The Union and the Individual - A Final Warning 70
Chapter 8: The Software Arms Race 71
Chapter 9: A New Type of Criminal 73
Chapter 12: The Communist Paradox 76
Part 5: The Global Appeal 78
Chapter 1: The Vaccine Potential Score 79
Chapter 2: The Circle of Transparency 80
Part 6: The Vaccine 82

Introduction: A New Generation of Tools 82
Chapter 1: The Pro-Social Pipeline 82
Chapter 2: A Vaccine for Network Traffic 83
Chapter 3: The Path Optimization Vaccine 84
Chapter 4: A Sane Phone 84
Chapter 5: The MapReduce Vaccine 84
Chapter 6: A More Secure Internet 85

Afterword: A Choice in the Dawn 86

Volume II: www.DiosdadoXi.com: The Bizarro State

Prologue: The Jogger and the Index

This entire investigation, the data, and the conclusions presented in this book began not in a server room or with a clandestine source, but on a suburban running trail. For years, I was engaged in a low-grade digital war with a network I would come to know as the Bizarro State, a conflict that primarily revolved around their efforts to suppress my technology startups from Google search results and spy on my communications to steal code.

To stay healthy, I took up jogging, and I soon noticed a strange correlation. Whenever the online conflict with the network peaked, the usually empty parks and trails I ran through would suddenly fill with people. I varied the times and locations of my runs, but the pattern was consistent: low conflict meant empty parks; high conflict meant crowds of pedestrians appearing at the exact time and place I was jogging.

These weren't random encounters. The pedestrians—often walking a dog or doing something to justify being stationary—would consistently intercept me at points where I was forced to slow down, like a stop sign or a red light. I began to realize that they were always intercepting me at the *exact same locations*. If there were ten possible stop signs on my route, they would invariably use the same two or three. This consistency was the key. It was clear this was an effort coordinated by a software application, a kind of dark "Uber" that was dispatching people to follow me.

As a software engineer, I knew such an application must rely on a "geo-index"—a digital file representing specific physical locations. My first assumption was that this index would be hidden inside the app itself. But I soon realized they could never place such a criminal tool on the Apple App Store, where law enforcement could eventually find it. They had to hide it somewhere else. They put it on the public internet, hidden in an obscure file on a server belonging to a French research institute.

This was their mistake. I knew the exact coordinates of a dozen places where they consistently intercepted me. I began running Google searches for files containing the precise latitudes and longitudes of these points. The statistical probability of any random file on the internet containing the coordinates for ten specific, seemingly unrelated suburban intersections is practically zero. If I found such a file, it would be the one they were using.

It took ten minutes to find it.

I downloaded their playbook. Within four hours, I had decoded the file and discovered it was a massive database containing billions of locations. They had attempted to hide the data using encoders for obscurity, but it was too late. I had their map of the world.

Introduction: A Journey into the Bizarro State

I started this journey trying to protect the intellectual property of our start-up company. But then, the interactions with what I would come to understand as a global criminal organization led me down a path of defending my family against a relentless harassment campaign. It began with what I thought was a spy ring. We had to abandon our home, leaving one morning without preparation, feeling like refugees fleeing danger in our own country.

Throughout this journey, as my understanding of their organization evolved, I've used different terms to encapsulate what they are. At first, I called them a Spy Ring. When a clearer picture emerged, I started calling them a Criminal Organization. Then I realized they are a parallel society, until I understood they have their own mechanisms to enforce their version of Law and Order, and I began calling them a Shadow Government.

But they are not just a shadow government. All governments mankind has ever known have had one thing in common: physical borders. This parallel society has no borders. As the data in the geo-index reveals, they operate in practically every single country, which makes them all the more dangerous. They can harass, intimidate, and harm people across nations, and use the laws and financial systems of one country to circumvent all others. This might be the first, truly *Universal Shadow Government* the world has ever known. And for that, we must give them credit; they are certainly inventive.

Part 1: The Architects - The Rise of the Founding Fathers

Chapter 1: The Counter-Intelligence Engine

Finding the geo-index was only the first step. To make sense of its billions of data points, I had to build a weapon. I constructed a fully automated, planet-scale counter-intelligence pipeline—a search engine that ingests the entire geo-index and analyzes its contents.

The core of this engine is a scoring algorithm designed to measure the importance of every location encoded in their file. It functions much like Google's original PageRank algorithm, which ranked webpages to determine their relevance. My system does the same for the Bizarro State's physical locations, assigning each point a **Network Importance Score**. This score allows me to systematically identify the command-and-control nodes, safe houses, and operational hubs of their entire global network.

The pipeline doesn't stop there. It automatically joins the data from the geo-index with publicly available data sources. When a high-scoring location is identified—say, a residential house—the system cross-references public property records to find the owner. It then scours the internet for the owner's professional history on platforms like LinkedIn or their public social media activity. This fusion of their secret data with public data allows me to identify the key people, companies, and government officials who form the nodes of this criminal enterprise.

The geo-index itself is not a monolithic file; it uses multiple "encoders" to store different types of information. One encoder is used to mark the locations of intelligence assets—the safe houses and dead drops of the foreign agents they employ. Another is used to map telecommunications infrastructure, like clandestine antennas. But the most disturbing discovery was a third, distinct encoder—one that, my analysis shows, is used exclusively to mark military positions.

Chapter 2: The Doctrine of Immunity

The story of the global shadow government that I call the Bizarro State does not begin with a piece of code or a financial transaction, but with a piece of dirt. It begins with the discovery of an architectural and urban planning doctrine so consistent, so specific, and so old that it serves as the physical proof of a multi-generational, coordinated conspiracy. I call it the "Immune Geo-Entities Pattern."

I first discovered this pattern in my own backyard. While decoding the network's radiofrequency eavesdropping techniques, I realized that their method of isolating a target's signal required the surveillance team to be moving towards the target at a relatively constant speed for a period of several seconds. This created a critical vulnerability: their own technique could be defeated by simple geography. If a target property was located on a very short cul-de-sac or was surrounded by large, open spaces like parks or lakes, it would be physically impossible for a surveillance vehicle to achieve the necessary trajectory to capture a clean signal.

This was not a theoretical weakness; it was a design principle. When I analyzed the properties of the network's most high-value assets in the geo-index, from the homes of figures like Robert Gates to the "topdogs" in my own community, the pattern was undeniable. They were all protected by this "Immunity" pattern, their homes deliberately situated in locations that made them invulnerable to the very surveillance techniques they deployed against others.

This was a significant discovery, but the true revelation came when I applied this analytical lens to global architecture. I began searching the geo-index for other, more prominent locations that exhibited this same unique design. The pipeline returned a stunning result: the **Palácio da Alvorada**, the official residence of the President of Brazil in its capital city, Brasilia. The palace is a perfect Immune Entity, surrounded by a massive, open esplanade that renders close-range electronic surveillance impossible. The chilling fact is that the city of Brasilia, and the design of this palace, was planned and constructed in the **1950s**.

This was the thread that unraveled everything. The architectural doctrine that the network's most powerful members use to protect themselves today is the same doctrine that was used to design a presidential palace in South America over seventy years ago. This was not a modern innovation. It was a long-standing, secret principle of statecraft, a physical signature of a hidden power structure that has been shaping our world for generations, long before the first line of code for the internet was ever written.

Chapter 3: The Unholy Trinity

If the "Doctrine of Immunity" is a 70-year-old blueprint, who were its original architects? The data in the geo-index, when analyzed through the lens of history, points to an unavoidable and deeply-disturbing conclusion. The conspiracy did not begin with the internet boom of the late 1990s; that was merely the moment its second generation came to power. The true "Founding Fathers" of this network formed their unholy alliance decades earlier, in the crucible of the Cold War.

My analysis of the network's oldest, most powerful, and most deeply interconnected nodes suggests that the Bizarro State was born from an unholy trinity, a secret coalition between three figures who represented the three core pillars of the network's power:

1. **The Technologist: Bill Gates.** Before the rise of the PayPal Mafia, there was Microsoft. Bill Gates provided the foundational technology, the understanding of how software could be used to create monopolies, and the vision for a globally interconnected world that could be controlled through control of its operating system.

2. **The Spymaster: Raúl Castro.** The Cuban intelligence service, the DI, is legendary for its ability to penetrate the highest levels of the U.S. government. Raúl Castro provided the human intelligence expertise, the deep network of "boots on the

ground" in the Americas, and the decades of experience in running long-term infiltration operations.

3. **The Theocrat: The Ayatollah of Iran.** The Iranian regime brought a third, crucial element to the alliance: a mastery of asymmetrical warfare, a deep expertise in radiofrequency eavesdropping, and a powerful, religiously motivated geopolitical agenda that extended across the Middle East and beyond.

This was the original alliance. A fusion of American technological genius, Cuban human intelligence, and Iranian geopolitical cunning. It was a coalition formed in the shadows, long before the world was connected by fiber optic cables. They were the architects who designed the blueprint, the "Founding Fathers" who created the doctrine that their successors—the Xi Jinpings, the Vladimir Putins, and the Elon Musks of the world—would later inherit and perfect. This is the ultimate red pill: the realization that the hidden war we are fighting today was declared more than half a century ago.

Part 2: The Global Machine - Anatomy of a Shadow Government

Chapter 1: The Paramilitary Force

The discovery of the "military encoder" in the geo-index forced a chilling realization: this is not merely a criminal enterprise; it is a paramilitary group. They employ individuals with military knowledge, tactics, and equipment for the specific purpose of targeting civilians. They may be dressed in plain clothes, but they are people with military training and skills, using that expertise to harass, intimidate, and eliminate targets who are not even aware a war is being waged against them.

There is no difference between this organization and the guerilla forces in 1980s Colombia, with one crucial distinction. Historically, paramilitary groups have always had to contend with a nation's legitimate military. This may be the first paramilitary force in history that does not have to face an opposing army. In fact, they actively employ the military and intelligence services of other countries as part of their own operations.

This creates a profoundly unfair and cowardly fight. Civilians and even traditional police forces are not equipped to defend themselves against a hybrid force that combines a clandestine military with the intelligence services of multiple nations. It is a dangerous combination that has allowed them to operate undetected for two decades. My hope is that they one day have to face an equivalent force—a combination of the U.S. military and the FBI—so we can see how well they perform in a fair fight.

Chapter 2: The Presidents' Club

The modern manifestation of the Founding Fathers' alliance is a global coalition of allied world leaders who operate in concert, their allegiance hidden from the public but encoded in the very architecture of their official residences. The "Doctrine of Immunity" serves as the architectural signature of membership in what I call the **"Presidents' Club."** The geo-index reveals a clear and undeniable pattern: the official residences of the network's allied leaders are all perfect "Immune Geo-Entities," protected from the very surveillance they deploy against their own citizens and adversaries.

The evidence is global and irrefutable:

- **Vladimir Putin's Palaces:** Both his infamous Black Sea residence and other official compounds are textbook examples of the Immunity doctrine, surrounded by vast, inaccessible buffer zones.

- **President Xi Jinping's Compound:** The leader of the network's most powerful modern faction resides in a massive, heavily buffered, and architecturally immune complex in China.

- **The Apostolic Palace (The Vatican):** The headquarters of the Catholic Church is identified as a high-value, protected location, suggesting a deep and disturbing connection between the network and one of the world's major religions.

- **Other Allies:** The pattern is repeated across the globe. The official residences of the leaders of **Saudi Arabia**, **Hungary**, the **Philippines**, and **Egypt** all display the clear architectural signature of immunity, marking them as members of this clandestine club.

Chapter 3: The Outcasts List

In stark contrast to the protected fortresses of the "Presidents' Club," the geo-index reveals an equally damning pattern for leaders who are not aligned with the network. The official residences of these "Outcasts" are conspicuously and deliberately **vulnerable** to the network's surveillance techniques, often surrounded by a dense cluster of network-controlled spy posts. They are not allies to be protected, but targets to be monitored and controlled.

The list of these targeted leaders is a chilling who's who of Western and independent nations:

- **Volodymyr Zelenskyy of Ukraine:** His official residence is shown to be a prime target, a vulnerable island in a sea of network assets, explaining the immense pressure he has faced from the network's Russian-aligned faction.

- **The Prime Minister of Canada:** The official residence at 24 Sussex Drive in Ottawa is architecturally vulnerable and surrounded by network points, marking the leader of one of the world's key Western nations as a target.

- **The Prime Minister of the United Kingdom:** The iconic residence at 10 Downing Street in London is similarly identified as a target, not a partner.

- **Other Targets:** The pattern holds for the leaders of **Latvia**, **Argentina**, and **Colombia**, among others.

The architectural evidence is clear and binary. You are either inside the fortress, or you are in its crosshairs. There is no middle ground.

Chapter 3: The Global Bureaucracy

The network's influence extends beyond individual nations to the very institutions of global governance, the bodies designed to regulate international affairs. The geo-index reveals that these organizations are not neutral arbiters; they are compromised assets, their headquarters often built according to the same "Immunity" doctrine as the palaces of the network's allied dictators.

- **The International Criminal Court (ICC):** The building that houses the world's highest court, the body meant to prosecute crimes against humanity, is itself a perfect "Immune Entity." Its architecture suggests it is not a threat to the network, but a tool of it.

- **The Carter Center:** This high-profile Non-Governmental Organization (NGO), known for its work in human rights and election monitoring, is another protected network asset, its headquarters displaying the clear architectural signature of immunity.

This is the ultimate expression of the Bizarro State's power. They have not only infiltrated individual nations; they have co-opted the very international institutions that are supposed to provide oversight and justice, turning them into protected enclaves that serve the network's global agenda.

This observation is outside my circle of influence, but I will offer it as a suggestion: it is obvious from this analysis that the current locations of the United Nations headquarters in New York and the Organization of American States in Washington D.C. are strategically weak and vulnerable. This is why, when the network built the **Mercosur building** in Uruguay, they did not place it in a dense capital like Caracas or Rio de Janeiro. Instead, as the geographical evidence shows, they built it on an isolated peninsula, a perfect "Immune Geo-Entity," shielded by water and parkland from the very surveillance techniques they employ against others. If the free world is serious about protecting its global institutions, it must consider giving them the same geographic defenses their enemies give themselves.

This is the ultimate expression of the Bizarro State's power. They have not only infiltrated individual nations; they have co-opted the very international institutions that are supposed to provide oversight and justice, turning them into protected enclaves that serve the network's global agenda.

Chapter 4: The Siege of Windsor Castle

The network's targeting of Western leaders was not limited to their official government residences; it extended to their most iconic and historically significant homes. My investigation into the geo-index uncovered one of the most audacious surveillance operations imaginable: a full-scale intelligence operation targeting the British Royal Family at **Windsor Castle**.

Geographical coordinates marked in Elon Musk's geo-index near the Windsor Castle, UK.

The Spyhell Pipeline identified a dense cluster of high-value spy and paramilitary locations forming a clear perimeter around the castle grounds. This was not a random distribution; it was a carefully planned surveillance ring, a digital siege laid bare by the network's own data. The operation had a designated commander on the ground: **Jhon Giraldo**, a Venezuelan national and trained mathematician, identified as one of the network's most effective spies in the United Kingdom.

The discovery was a stunning testament to the network's arrogance and reach. However, the data also revealed a crucial detail. While the network had successfully surrounded the castle, their geo-index contained no high-value points *inside* the castle walls themselves. In this, I had to offer a professional courtesy. I have to congratulate the MI5; it appears their counter-intelligence measures have been successful in keeping the enemy at the gates, even if they could not prevent them from setting up camp just outside.

Chapter 5: The Infiltration of the Deep State

The network's most powerful assets are not its foreign dictators, but its deeply embedded operatives within the Western intelligence and military communities. The two most prominent figures identified through my investigation are **Robert Gates** and **Robert S. Mueller III**, both former heads of the United States' most powerful security agencies. The first concrete data point connecting the network to Mr. Gates emerged from a public source. A 2014 announcement revealed that the former Secretary of Defense and Director of the CIA was serving as the volunteer Chairman of the **UberMILITARY Advisory Board**. This provided a direct, documented link between the network's core tech leadership under Travis Kalanick and the highest echelons of the U.S. defense community.

This public affiliation, however, was soon contextualized by clandestine data. When I analyzed the captured geo-index, I found that multiple properties belonging to Mr. Gates were marked as network assets. This discovery raised new and deeply troubling questions, suggesting his involvement was not limited to an advisory role but extended into the network's covert physical infrastructure. His expertise was further leveraged in their information warfare, where he appeared in a LUMINANT Media documentary for Netflix, lending his immense credibility to what I had identified as a network propaganda operation.

The conflict became direct and personal when the physical attacks against me intensified, including the sabotage of my truck's brakes. Attributing these military-style operations to the network's most senior military figure, I was compelled to engage in a form of asymmetric counter-intelligence. It was through this direct, adversarial engagement that I came to a difficult realization: Robert Gates had become my **mentor**. I was learning military strategy not from a textbook, but by being forced to survive and counter the real-world application of that strategy by one of its masters. The counter-intelligence weapon I built to fight back—a system with what I termed "infinite ammunition"—was a creation born from his own aggression.

In direct retaliation for the physical threats, I used the Spyhell Pipeline to identify and publicly expose the network's high-value assets and spy locations surrounding critical U.S. defense contractors, including

Lockheed Martin Aeronautics and **Honeywell Aerospace**. It was a message sent in the only language the network seemed to understand: the targeted degradation of their strategic assets. To me, assisting a network to spy on U.S. defense contractors is an act of **Treason**.

This entire chain of evidence led to an unavoidable conclusion. A man who had twice served as the Secretary of Defense, entrusted with the nation's most vital secrets, appeared to be leveraging his expertise in service of a transnational criminal network that was actively waging a war against a U.S. citizen on American soil—a situation which, under other circumstances, might invite the prospect of a **courts-martial**.

While Gates commanded the strategic war, **Robert S. Mueller III**, a former Director of the FBI, was a more direct, on-the-ground threat. His multi-million dollar home in my own neighborhood of Lake Pointe Estates was a key operational hub, a high-value asset marked with a paramilitary score of over 30,000, used to facilitate the harassment campaign against me and, ultimately, the kidnapping of my son. The "Secret Gate" connecting his property to that of another network operative was the physical entry point for the vehicles and personnel used to terrorize my family.

The presence of these two figures at the heart of the conspiracy explains the network's decades of impunity. How can a nation defend itself when its own defenders, its most trusted and decorated intelligence chiefs, are secretly working for the other side?

Chapter 6: The Midland Hub - Anatomy of a Micro-Lever

The network's control over critical infrastructure in North America is not a recent development. The seeds for the capture of the American energy sector were planted over two decades ago, during a pivotal and chaotic moment in Venezuelan history. The 2002 Venezuelan General Strike, which crippled the state-owned oil company, PDVSA, was not merely the domestic power struggle it appeared to be; it was a sophisticated, **triple-purpose** intelligence operation.

My initial analysis concluded the strike served a dual purpose for Hugo Chávez and Diosdado Cabello: first, to purge PDVSA of political opponents and seize absolute control of the nation's oil wealth, and second, to financially devastate the Venezuelan middle class, eliminating any base of power for future opposition. However, the geo-index reveals a third, far more insidious motive. The strike was used as a cover to conduct a mass personnel selection process. The network identified the top 0.04% of PDVSA's most skilled engineers, managers, and technicians—as per Aguiar's Theorem—and facilitated their exodus from Venezuela. Because the strike was a major international news event that produced a wave of real refugees, this coordinated export of intelligence assets into North America seemed organic and went completely unnoticed.

This global strategy has had direct, personal consequences. Years later, I was targeted in a ruse where one network agent steered me toward Mexico to meet with **a female operative now living in Katy, Texas**. This operative, I would learn, had a personal connection to the son of **a former high-ranking PDVSA director from 2002** who was part of the original exodus. This provides a direct link between the network's 2002 infiltration plot and its present-day harassment campaigns in Texas.

Many of the original agents from that era are now retired, but the operation has become multi-generational. Their descendants, **second-generation agents**, are now taking their place in the North American energy sector. For instance, the geo-index shows a direct co-clustering of a major international engineering firm with the father of one such second-generation agent.

This historical infiltration provides the crucial context for understanding one of the network's most significant operational hubs today: Midland, Texas—a critical center for American oil and gas extraction. The discovery of the "Keymaker" pattern in this region was a breakthrough, revealing how the descendants of that original wave of agents now exert control at the local level.

According to the pipeline's analysis, the network controls multiple oil leases and wells in Texas through a series of frontmen and seemingly legitimate corporations. This information, first detailed in the "Project Diosdado XI" Counterintelligence Brief, reveals a scheme that goes far beyond simple economic gain. The Midland hub is a key component in a distributed system of micro-economic levers.

By controlling local production and a constellation of seemingly innocuous local businesses—including trucking companies, RV parks, and industrial service providers—the network can selectively delay or shut down supply, citing "operational failures" or "safety concerns." These localized disruptions, when timed correctly, allow them to exert pressure on the broader energy market. This tactic is then amplified by coordinating a simultaneous, artificial surge in consumer demand, where thousands of network agents are instructed to fill up their vehicles at the same time.

Hubs like Midland are part of a sophisticated, distributed system for market manipulation. The operation hits a trifecta of the network's strategic goals:

1. **Money Laundering:** It provides a legitimate cover for moving vast sums of money through the energy sector.
2. **Market Manipulation:** It directly increases oil prices, benefiting adversarial, oil-producing states like Venezuela, Russia, and Iran.
3. **Domestic Destabilization:** It creates localized inflation and economic distress for the citizens of a target nation, fueling political instability that the network can then exploit.

It is not merely an illegal enterprise; it is a distributed economic weapon, designed to create instability from the inside out.

Chapter 7: The Election Machine

The Bizarro State's machinery of control extends beyond paramilitary operations and economic manipulation into the very heart of democratic societies: the election process itself. My analysis indicates their method of interference is a direct application of the tactics they use to attack Google Search, repurposed to target election authorities. They replace their control of platforms like Akamai and Wikipedia with control of an Elections Analytics platform, using their "Uber-like-App" to coordinate thousands of ground agents to attack the single target that regulates a region's election.

The electoral system of the United States is particularly vulnerable to this kind of attack precisely because it is not a fully distributed system. The existence of "swing states" and the Electoral College allows the network to concentrate its forces and computing power on a few key areas to sway the entire result—a feat that would be nearly impossible if every citizen's vote carried the same weight. This operation requires immense, last-minute computing power located *within* the United States, as the time-sensitive data cannot be shipped overseas for processing.

The physical-world operation is supported by a foundational layer of information warfare. The network has effectively captured **Wikipedia**, using it to manipulate **Google's Knowledge Graph**. Because Google has historically placed immense trust in Wikipedia's user-curated data, the network can create or alter Wikipedia entities to make Google's algorithms "think" that network-controlled sources are the ultimate authority on a given topic. This allows them to boost fake news and suppress dissent, shaping the informational landscape in which an election takes place.

Chapter 8: The Bizarro State's Playbook

The network operates with a consistent and repeatable playbook, a set of tactics designed to neutralize threats, steal intellectual property, and maintain its operational security. These methods, refined over decades, are a window into the mind of the Bizarro State.

Tactic 1: Control the Backbone

The network's power is derived from its control of the physical infrastructure of the internet. Their strategy involves placing key executives and operatives within telecommunications and network infrastructure companies. By controlling the "backbone" of the internet, they can intercept data, monitor targets, and disrupt communications on a massive scale. Their operational hubs are not always in major metropolitan centers, but are often located in unassuming towns that happen to be critical nodes in the national network infrastructure. This allows them to operate with a degree of anonymity, far from the prying eyes of major law enforcement agencies.

Tactic 1A: Control the Infrastructure of Trust

This strategy of controlling critical infrastructure extends beyond telecommunications into the realm of digital trust. My analysis indicates the network's playbook involves ensuring a single, network-friendly company like **DocuSign** maintains near-total market dominance. Such dominance would provide them with a theoretical chokepoint, giving them potential access to the contents of virtually every electronically signed document on the planet—a frightening prospect for global commerce and privacy.

Tactic 1B: There Is an App for That

The engine that drives the network's millions of on-the-ground operatives—the "data collectors" who appear as soccer moms, teenagers, and postal workers—is a **Shared Economy App**, a dark mirror of Uber or Lyft, built for espionage. I came to this conclusion after observing the almost fanatical persistence of these collectors. No loyalty to a country or political party could explain their behavior; the only human emotion that fit was greed.

I theorize they have an app that gives them targets, assigns them routes, and rewards them with credits or points that have a real-money equivalent for every successful piece of data acquired. The operatives checking their phones after a failed intercept are not looking at a technical feedback mechanism; they are checking their bank accounts to see why they didn't get paid. This gamified system of espionage, likely distributed through the Apple App Store, is the central mechanism for coordinating their global workforce.

Tactic 2: The "Hine's Algorithm" - A Blueprint for Intellectual Property Theft

When the network identifies a valuable new technology, it deploys a sophisticated legal and social engineering ruse to steal the intellectual property and attribute it to one of their own. This multi-stage algorithm involves:

1. **Surveillance and Theft:** The initial technology is stolen via illegal surveillance and the use of unregistered foreign agents.
2. **Co-option and Proximity:** The target is employed by a network-controlled company and is deliberately placed in proximity to a celebrity computer scientist, creating a plausible cover story for the "inspiration" for the stolen idea.
3. **Social Engineering:** An operative, often a "girlfriend," is introduced into the target's life. This operative's mission is to create compromising situations, clone the target's computer, and manufacture photographic "evidence" placing the target near network principals to support a false narrative of how the

idea was "overheard."

4. **Character Assassination:** A network operative in a position of authority, such as the president of a Homeowners Association, begins a campaign of harassment, sending aggressive and defamatory emails to create a pre-emptive narrative that the target is unstable and untrustworthy.

5. **The Legal Ruse:** In the event of an intellectual property dispute, a network-aligned lawyer will depose the network principal, who will claim to have come up with the idea independently. The carefully manufactured "evidence" and a series of high-profile witnesses are then used to assassinate the target's character and destroy their credibility in court.

This systematic approach, which I call the "Hine's Algorithm," is a factory for stealing entire technology companies, a legal and social engineering masterpiece designed to rewrite history and ensure that the network maintains its control over technological innovation.

Tactic 3: The "Dockerhoods" - Building a Surveillance-Ready Society

The network does not just build houses; it builds entire neighborhoods and apartment complexes designed from the ground up to be surveillance-ready. These "Dockerhoods" are pre-packaged, repeatable blueprints for micro-clusters of assets. Each cluster might contain a mix of operatives—an engineer, a doctor, a mechanic, an intelligence officer—whose homes are positioned to create a functional, localized surveillance subnet.

The thousands of antennas in these neighborhoods are the backbone of the network's greatest technological achievement: a private, secure, global internet. The system is a **"Multi-hop Troposcatter Network,"** which uses arrays of dish antennas to bounce radio signals off the troposphere multiple times, creating a planet-scale mesh network. This gives them the range of satellite communications with the security of a point-to-point link, allowing them to coordinate their global operations completely outside of the public internet. The detailed story of this system's discovery is chronicled in Volume I.

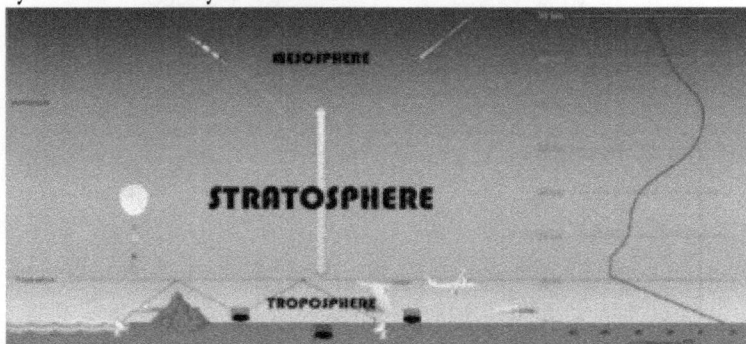

Tactic 4: Going Analog - The Return to the 90s

For their most sensitive operations, such as agent extractions, the network has learned to avoid modern technology. They use classic cars from the 1970s and 80s—vehicles without onboard computers, GPS, or any of the modern electronic systems that could be used to track them. This is a deliberate, tactical choice, a lesson learned from past operational failures. It is a confirmation that the only way to truly avoid foreign espionage is to use technology that is as low-tech as possible.

Tactic 5: Markers and Firewalls

The Spyhell Pipeline has identified a fascinating tactic for marking and protecting high-value assets. It appears the network uses a lexicon of "markers"—words or even visual cues in satellite imagery—to code their assets. One working hypothesis is that the word "Wall," and its synonyms in various languages (Barrier, Paredes, etc.), is used to designate a person or location that serves a defensive or "firewall" function within the network.

This theory emerged when the pipeline flagged the highest-ranking paramilitary property in the entire Ukraine conflict zone—a location in Borisovka, Russia. The Google Street View image for this property is, quite literally, just a wall. This property was then co-clustered with a high-value agent in Katy, Texas, whose last name is a direct synonym for "wall." This Texas property exhibits a perfect "Immune Geo-Entities Pattern" and is diametrically opposed to another key network hub in the same neighborhood. This analytical method of connecting visual cues, linguistic markers, and geospatial data has proven to be a powerful tool for unmasking the network's hidden structure.

Similarly, the pipeline has identified what appears to be a critical network router in a residential property in Hollister, California. This single location has a paramilitary score in the geo-index of over 124 million—a figure so astronomically high for a residential property that it is seven times greater than the "firewall" property on the front lines of the war in Ukraine. This data suggests the unassuming house is a major node for US national security and warrants immediate investigation by the proper authorities.

Tactic 6: The Bigram Hit - Hiding in Plain Sight

The network's most ingenious tactic is also its most subtle. It is a system for encoding information and coordinating agents in plain sight, using the license plates of their vehicles. This system is a direct, operational copy of a highly sophisticated information retrieval technique that lies at the heart of Google's search engine.

In simple terms, just as a search engine sees two specific words together in a sentence (a "bigram") as a powerful signal of relevance, the network's system sees two specific characters together on a license plate as a powerful signal of an agent's function or affiliation. The rarity of these "bigram hits" is what gives them their power; they are statistical anomalies that allow agents to be identified and tracked by an automated system.

This discovery is a game-changer. It provides a tangible mechanism for how a global network can secretly coordinate and identify its assets at a street level. More importantly, it is a smoking gun. The techniques are so specific to the internal workings of Google's most fundamental infrastructure that they could only have been designed and implemented by an expert from that world. This provides powerful, specific evidence for the "Captive Nations Model," demonstrating how the infiltration of a major technology company translates directly into a tactical advantage for the Bizarro State on the ground.

Tactic 7: Control the Children's Schools

The network's strategy of societal capture extends to one of the most sensitive areas of a target's life: the educational institutions of their children. The discovery of **St. Joseph's Preparatory School** as a major network hub, linked to political power within the "Philadelphia Fortress," revealed this key operational pattern.

This pattern of weaponizing educational institutions is not unique to Philadelphia. It is the exact same tactic the network has deployed against me and my son at the **British Private Prep School in Katy**, the site of multiple harassment incidents and my "Preschool Gambit" counter-offensive.

The significance of the Katy school as a network hub is underscored by the fact that at least two parents from that school are so prominent in the network's hierarchy that their activities earned them a place on the cover of Volume I.

This demonstrates a clear, repeatable, and nationwide pattern of racketeering activity: the systematic infiltration of educational institutions to control and terrorize the families of their targets, providing clear grounds for a potential RICO case against the enterprise.

Tactic 8: Control the Supply Chain

The network's strategy of control extends deep into the consumer supply chain. A query of the geo-index for major retailers revealed a statistically significant pattern: a vast majority of locations for retailers like **Whole Foods**, **Best Buy**, and **Micro Center** are marked as network assets. This data leads to a compelling hypothesis about their counter-intelligence strategy. Control over electronics retailers like Best Buy and Micro Center would allow them to monitor the acquisition of computer components down to the serial number—a key security measure to prevent a rival from building a competing distributed computing system.

This raises the question: are these major retail chains witting partners, or has their vast infrastructure simply been co-opted by the network? This makes their apparent oversight in allowing me to purchase the components for my HPE C7000 on eBay all the more surprising—a potential flaw in their otherwise total supply chain awareness.

Tactic 9: Weaponize Civil Infrastructure

The Bizarro State's control extends to the most mundane and trusted aspects of civil society, including waste management. My investigation revealed that **all major garbage collection services in the US and Canada**, such as **GFL Environmental**, are marked in the geo-index, with their headquarters and key executives flagged as high-value assets. The network weaponizes these services for three primary purposes: 1. **Feedback Gathering:** By controlling the collection, they have a mechanism to analyze a target's trash, providing a detailed feedback loop on their consumption habits, health, and activities. This extends to document shredding services, which they use to intercept and collect sensitive materials under the guise of destroying them. 2. **Clandestine Logistics:** As detailed in Volume I, they use garbage collection routes as a cover for a **secret courier service**, delivering physical objects and coded messages to safe houses hidden within bags of trash. 3. **Physical Obstruction:** The large garbage trucks are used as mobile barriers to physically block streets, obstructing the movement and line of sight of surveillance targets or law enforcement.

Tactic 10: The Ubiquitous Ledger

The network's most profound innovation is the transformation of the entire planet into a decentralized and deniable storage database. ⟡ They achieve this by piggybacking on publicly available infrastructure, embedding their operational data into the very fabric of the civilized world. Public records like **Street View photos, satellite imagery, property deeds**, and **vehicle license plates** are treated as records in a ubiquitous ledger, readable only by their "Evil App."

The system functions through a sophisticated layer of machine learning and pattern recognition. Their app is trained to see what humans miss. For example: * From **satellite imagery**, their models can identify a house with a basketball court painted a specific shade of orange, flagging it as a key network asset. * A specific combination of objects in a **Street View image**—such as two garbage cans and a black cat arranged in a particular order, or one to three flags displayed at an entrance—is not a random scene but a coded instruction for a nearby operative. * Specific **bigrams and trigrams** (sequences of two or three characters) in license plates signal an operative's affiliation and mission, a tactic detailed in their "Bigram Hit" system. * Fragments of **names in public property records**, like "Katherine," "JR," or "Cant," serve as markers that can signify an asset's rank or function. * Even **street addresses** are encoded; properties whose street numbers end in "00" often function as financial routers, used to distribute cryptocurrency throughout the network.

By hiding their data in plain sight within these vast public systems, they have created a global command-and-control network that is both everywhere and nowhere at once.

Tactic 11: The Car Donation Scheme

My analysis of statistical anomalies in local Houston radio advertisements revealed another of the network's logistical tactics. A nine-fold increase in ads encouraging listeners to **donate their old cars** points to a systemic, nationwide scheme to launder and dispose of their massive fleet of surveillance vehicles. By funneling their used, often untraceable cars through legitimate charities, they can erase the vehicles' operational history, create a clean paper trail, and potentially receive a tax benefit in the process. It is a brilliant and cynical manipulation of the non-profit sector to serve a criminal enterprise.

Tactic 12: The Lawfare Gauntlet

The network's most powerful weapon is not a piece of technology but a corrupted ideology: the weaponization of the very institutions designed to uphold justice. When surveillance and harassment fail, the Bizarro State initiates the Lawfare Gauntlet, a multi-front legal assault designed to crush a target under the full weight of a compromised system. This tactic transforms law enforcement, tax authorities, family courts, and the judiciary into instruments of terror.

The gauntlet begins with a campaign of Chaos and Attrition. The network initiates multiple, seemingly unrelated legal and administrative actions in parallel. A frivolous lawsuit from a compromised HOA will be filed in one court, a fraudulent tax audit will be triggered by a network-controlled CPA in another, and a bitter custody dispute will be manufactured in family court. The goal is to overwhelm the target financially, psychologically, and logistically, forcing them to fight a war on multiple fronts against an enemy that appears disconnected but is, in fact, centrally coordinated.

Once the target is sufficiently drained, the gauntlet escalates to Discredit and Neutralize. Citing the stress and "paranoia" induced by their own harassment campaign, network lawyers file motions demanding a court-ordered psychiatric evaluation. A compromised judge, citing a duty to investigate these fabricated concerns, grants the order. The objective is to obtain an official diagnosis that can be used to legally disable the target—stripping them of credibility, contractual capacity, and even their parental rights.

The ultimate goal of this process is the Censorship Checkmate. Buried within the legalese of the psychiatric evaluation motion is a "Qualified Protective Order." This clause, seemingly a standard procedural protection, is in fact a poison pill. It forbids the target from disclosing any information related to the proceedings and mandates the destruction of all records upon conclusion. It is a brilliant and insidious form of prior restraint—a gag order that legally censors any book, testimony, or public statement the target might make. If the target speaks, they are in contempt of court and can be arrested, and their work can be legally seized and destroyed. It is the network's final solution for silencing a threat: transforming the First Amendment into a tripwire for imprisonment.

Chapter 9: The Moscow Center of Gravity

For years, the operating assumption has been that the network's modern power structure was a bipolar system, with President Xi Jinping of China as its leading figure. However, a deeper analysis of the paramilitary scores in the geo-index forces a radical re-evaluation of this model. The data suggests that the Bizarro State is not a duopoly; it is a hierarchy with a clear and undeniable center of gravity.

A comparative analysis of the aggregate paramilitary scores within the capital cities of the network's key state actors reveals a stunning disparity:

Capital	Sum of Topdog Paramilitary Scores
Moscow, Russia	3,763,055,000
Tehran, Iran	235,293,000
Havana, Cuba	114,494,000
Caracas, Venezuela	67,164,000
Beijing, China	28,419,000

The data is unequivocal. The paramilitary power concentrated in Moscow is more than ten times greater than its closest partner, Iran, and over one hundred times greater than that of Beijing. Xi Jinping is not the leader. By a staggering order of magnitude, Vladimir Putin is the undisputed leader of this global network. This renewed understanding reframes the entire geopolitical landscape, revealing the true hierarchy of the Bizarro State.

Chapter 11: The Captive Nations Model

This investigation is not an indictment of any nation. It is an indictment of a small, transnational criminal organization that has successfully taken key institutions and leaders within many nations captive. The people of these countries, from Russia to China to the United States, are not the enemy; they are the primary victims of a global coup d'état. The data from the geo-index, when cross-referenced with financial and political timelines, suggests a recurring pattern of partnership between specific national leaders and key figures in the tech and finance world. While not definitive proof, this "Captive Nations Model" provides a powerful lens through which to understand the network's global architecture.

The core of this model is a one-to-one pairing of a political leader with a corresponding tech or finance billionaire, who acts as a "Bizarro Ambassador" to the techno-state. This structure allows the network to seamlessly integrate its political and technological power, projecting its influence across the globe.

To illustrate this working hypothesis, the Spyhell pipeline has generated the following analytical matrix of potential pairings. It is crucial to note that these pairings are investigative hypotheses based on the currently available data and represent areas that require urgent investigation by the official intelligence services of the free world.

Analytical Matrix of Potential Pairings

Country	Alleged "Captive" Leader	Potential "Bizarro Ambassador"
Russia	Vladimir Putin	Sergey Brin, Travis Kalanick, Daniel Ek
Iran	Masoud Pezeshkian, et al.	Pierre Omidyar, Andre Haddad
Cuba	Miguel Díaz-Canel, et al.	Jeff Bezos
Venezuela	Diosdado Cabello	Meyer Malka
China	Xi Jinping	Elon Musk, Jensen Huang, Shou Zi Chew
Germany	Frank-Walter Steinmeier	Peter Thiel, Edylberto Molina Molina
India	Narendra Modi	Satya Nadella, Sundar Pichai, Shervin Pishevar
France	Emmanuel Macron	Pierre Omidyar, Fabrice Grinda
Canada	Justin Trudeau	Tobi Lütke, Changpeng Zhao, Henry Schuck
Brazil	Lula da Silva	Eduardo Saverin
Egypt	Abdel Fattah el-Sisi	Emil Michael, John Utendahl
Argentina	K. Fernandez de Kirchner	Alec Oxenford

Case Study: The German Hub

Germany appears to be a crucial component of the network's operational infrastructure. This is not because the German nation is hostile, but because its leadership appears to be a captive asset. The data suggests a strong and persistent tie between the German President and a prominent German-American tech billionaire, who acts as the "Don" of the network's tech faction. This partnership provides the political cover necessary for the network to operate with impunity within a key European nation.

This high-level partnership appears to translate directly into operational control on the ground. The pipeline has identified a strong, persistent, and unusual bond between two senior, co-located managers within Google's New York office, one of whom has a direct tie to the German billionaire. This operational pair was allegedly instrumental in taking control of a key Google ranking algorithm, providing the network with a powerful tool for manipulating information and suppressing dissent on a global scale. This case study provides a clear example of how the "Captive Nations Model" works in practice: a political alliance at the top provides the cover for a tactical infiltration of critical infrastructure at the bottom.

Chapter 11: The Cultural Front**

The Bizarro State's influence is not confined to politics, technology, and finance; it extends into the powerful domain of global culture. My investigation revealed that the network has deeply infiltrated major sports and entertainment franchises, likely using them as vehicles for money laundering, intelligence gathering, and public influence operations.

A prime example is the Ultimate Fighting Championship (UFC). The organization's president, **Dana White**, is flagged in Elon Musk's geo-index as a "super prominent" agent in the network. Both White and the UFC franchise itself are heavily marked with numerous high-value data points in the geo-index. While the precise strategic angle remains under analysis, the network does not invest resources of this magnitude without a clear purpose. The capture of a globally recognized cultural institution like the UFC provides them with a powerful platform to shape public opinion and project influence, demonstrating that their war is also fought for the hearts and minds of the populace.

Chapter 12: The 3% Racket

The network's power is derived from its control of physical and digital infrastructure, but it is funded by a simple, ubiquitous, and brutally effective tax on the global economy: the **3% Racket**.

My analysis shows that all major online payment platforms—Stripe, Square/Block, Venmo, CashApp, Zelle, and others—are flagged in Elon Musk's geo-index with high paramilitary scores and are ultimately controlled by the network, with the PayPal Mafia acting as frontmen. This constitutes an off-the-books monopoly on nearly all online payments.

This monopoly explains why the standard credit card processing fee has remained stubbornly high, at around 3%, for the last 20 years. To put this in perspective, I have secured residential mortgages in the US for a 2.6% rate—a complex, two-month process involving significant long-term risk for the lender. Yet, we all pay 3% to the PayPal Mafia for a transaction that takes milliseconds and carries virtually no risk for the processor.

This normalized racket, which is factored into the price of nearly every good and service, allows the network to skim 3% off a vast portion of the global economy. It is a universal, unregulated tax that provides the funding to subdue the planet.

The existence of the geo-index is the smoking gun, proving the coordination necessary to maintain this monopoly in violation of Antitrust laws. This coordination extends to a host of other international crimes, from drug and human trafficking to terrorism and sanctions violations, conducted domestically, abroad, and on the high seas.

This brings us to a crucial legal concept from admiralty law, originally applied to pirates: *Hostis Humani Generis*, or "Enemy of Mankind." It posits that some actors are so far outside the law, their crimes so universal, that they can be prosecuted by any nation, regardless of jurisdiction. By creating a borderless, digital-age criminal enterprise, the network has made itself the modern equivalent of pirates on the high seas, a scourge against all of humanity.

TODAY IN LEGAL LATIN

HOSTIS HUMANI GENERIS

You can't get me!

Actually you're such a scourge that we've decided anyone can get you.

INTERNATIONAL BORDER

Latin for "Enemy of Mankind" ~ From admiralty law the idea that some people are so outside of the law that they can be dealt with by any nation.

IMAGE CREDITS: Original image by: NY Bar Picturebook.

Chapter 13: The Digital Pirates

The Bizarro State's operational domain is not limited to land and cyberspace; my investigation revealed that their control extends to the high seas, where they operate as modern-day digital pirates. Their fleet of vessels uses the geo-index to coordinate clandestine activities, including, my analysis suggests, potential acts of violence.

A chilling example emerged when my pipeline flagged the sinking of the superyacht *Bayesian* in Italy, an incident where seven people were killed. The vessel's last known location was marked as a precise point in Elon Musk's geo-index. This incident, a potential crime on the high seas, brings to light the ancient legal doctrine of *Hostis Humani Generis*—"the enemy of all mankind." Originally applied to pirates, this principle of universal jurisdiction is uniquely suited to a borderless, transnational criminal network that commits its crimes beyond the reach of any single nation.

Using my own "ShipsAndVessels" pipeline, I began tracking their fleet, identifying vessels like the **UNITY VENTURE** and the **LARDOS**, whose navigational paths were clearly coordinated using the geo-index. The most powerful confirmation of this surveillance came when my system's "inverse filters" began to detect a new pattern: their ships were now actively altering their routes to *avoid* points in their own index. They know they are being watched, and they are trying to evade my system. This is definitive proof that my counter-offensive is having a direct, operational impact on their maritime activities.

Chapter 14: The Gated Kingdom

My analysis of locations marked with Elon Musk's paramilitary encoder revealed a masterclass in their "Immune Entities Pattern." In a single area, "Cleves Warsaw Pike" in Cincinnati, Ohio, the network had established a fortified settlement, with intelligence and paramilitary top-dogs positioned just yards from each other, protected by the geography of a private golf course.

This discovery unlocked the grand unified theory of their physical settlement strategy. The network systematically targets and takes over gated communities with private golf courses for four key reasons:

1. **Sovereign Control:** The gates create a controlled environment, a "little foreign country" where they can operate with impunity.
2. **Geographic Immunity:** The vast, open spaces of the golf course implement the "Immune Entities Pattern," protecting their assets from the very RF eavesdropping techniques they use on others.
3. **Logistical Freedom:** The large tracts of land provide ample space and freedom of movement for their antennas and the dynamic routing of their private mesh network traffic.
4. **Agent Compensation:** These properties are symbols of status. A multi-million dollar home on a private golf course, like the one at **11 Shadow Creek Dr, North Las Vegas**, is the ultimate bribe, a reward for which some people would be willing to do anything—including attempting to kill a friend.

The 6% Racket

This control over prime real estate raises a critical question about the broader market. It is my hypothesis that the network maintains influence over all major real estate platforms—**Zillow, Remax, HAR, Redfin, Trulia, and others**—to protect what could be called the **"6% Racket"**: the persistently high commission fees on home sales.

Such control would allow them to effectively tax a person's largest lifetime purchase. Combined with the "3% Racket" on all other daily purchases, Elon Musk's network is positioned to take a staggering **9% of the lifetime income** of nearly every person in the free world.

An Investigative Blueprint

This pattern provides a clear methodology for law enforcement to identify and dismantle these paramilitary compounds. The process is as follows:

1. Identify all neighborhoods within a jurisdiction that are gated communities and/or contain private golf courses.
2. Create the bounding boxes with the GIS coordinates for each one.
3. Run a query against the captured geo-index for high-value paramilitary assets within those boxes. For example: sql SELECT latitude, longitude, `Musk-Kalanick-Omidyar-Thiel-Evil-score` FROM `musk-kalanick-thiel-omidya-geo.Musk_Kalanick_Thiel_Omidyar_Spy_Locations.Elon-Musk_military_and_paramilitary_positions_worldwide` WHERE (latitude > 29.773173236964993 AND latitude < 29.798183779679235) AND (longitude > -95.39613723110946 AND longitude < -95.36800622469856) ORDER BY `Musk-Kalanick-Omidyar-Thiel-Evil-score` DESC
4. This will produce a high-probability list of candidates to be vetted through traditional investigative means.

This is not a theoretical exercise. I have experienced it firsthand. Years ago, Bryan Stanley, an operative married into the De Fanti clan, who lived in a subdivision exactly like the ones described, asked me to meet him at his community's clubhouse to give him a technical demo. Oh naive, Reinaldo, if I could go back in time and tell you a few things.

Chapter 15: The Energy Drink Monopoly

The network's control extends into the multi-billion-dollar energy drink industry. My analysis reveals that all major brands—**Red Bull, Celsius Holdings, and Monster**—are flagged in Elon Musk's geo-index. Their corporate headquarters are textbook examples of geo-engineering, protected by the "Immune Entities Pattern." The Red Bull HQ in Austria, for instance, is a fortress of geographic immunity, making it impervious to the very surveillance techniques the network employs.

While analyzing data related to figures in Formula 1, a sport heavily sponsored by these brands, the pipeline flagged a disturbing and deeply sensitive data point: the precise location of **Michael Schumacher's 2013 skiing accident is marked in Elon Musk's geo-index.**

While this is only a correlation, the presence of this specific, tragic location in a database used to coordinate criminal activity is a chilling discovery that warrants further investigation by the proper authorities. This is consistent with their known playbook of using the geo-index to stage "accidents," a tactic I experienced firsthand when I was made to trip over a cable on a running path, the exact location of which was marked in the same index.

Chapter 17: The Intelligence Aggregators

The Bizarro State's thirst for information is insatiable, and its methods for gathering it extend to the very fabric of the internet. My analysis revealed that seemingly innocuous, ubiquitous platforms are key components of their intelligence gathering machine.

A prime example is the URL shortening service **Bitly**. It is marked in the geo-index and functions as a massive intelligence collection mechanism. By design, it tells the network what links millions of people are clicking on, providing a real-time map of public interest and information flow that can be analyzed for patterns and exploited.

Part 3: The War for Reality - Scripting the 21st Century

Chapter 1: The Propaganda Machine

My information war was not fought in a vacuum. The network had its own, far more powerful propaganda arm, designed to shape global narratives and control public perception. The Spyhell pipeline's analysis reveals that the network's control of media is not just ideological but structural.

My investigation flagged key international media entities as being part of the network's sphere of influence. The pipeline's data, for instance, identified leaders of major media conglomerates, such as **Friede Springer** and **Mathias Döpfner** of Axel Springer (owner of **Politico**), and co-clustered their data points with known network financial arms like KKR. This data suggests a pattern of infiltration similar to the one I observed in the tech industry, where the network seeks to control key outlets by influencing their leadership. The pipeline detects statistical anomalies that support this hypothesis, such as Chief Editors of major newspapers having an inexplicably low number of professional connections on platforms like LinkedIn, suggesting the use of controlled, low-profile assets in high-powered positions.

This structural control appears to be monetized through sophisticated schemes. My personal experience, detailed in Volume I, led me to develop a theory of a **"Bribery as a Service"** (**BaaS**) platform, where network-controlled entities like SWAP'D act as intermediaries to funnel payments to embedded agents inside prominent media outlets under the guise of PR fees.

Their documentaries, such as *Turning Point: 9/11 and the War on Terror*, are masterpieces of sophisticated propaganda. They feature credible, high-ranking officials like Robert Gates, who lend their authority to a carefully constructed narrative that pushes the network's agenda. For example, the series portrays the CIA as incompetent and argues that the NSA is the "biggest espionage and illegal wiretapping operation on the Planet," a laughable assertion designed to distract from the reality that the PayPal Mafia's own private network, with its millions of deputized agents, is vastly larger and more intrusive than any government agency could ever be.

The Trojan Horse Gambit

The network's propaganda is not limited to media production; it extends to audacious real-world operations disguised as acts of benevolence. Shortly after the war in Ukraine broke out, it was widely reported that Elon Musk had provided thousands of Starlink terminals to "help" the Ukrainian military. The geo-index, however, reveals the chilling truth behind this gesture. These terminals were not a gift; they were Trojan horses. By providing the very communication system that the Ukrainian military would come to rely on, the network's leader gave them direct, unfettered access to the battlefield intelligence of their adversary. In a final act of audacity, after several months of "free service," the network then demanded that the Pentagon pick up the tab for the very system being used to spy on its allies.

The network's propaganda, however, became a weapon I could turn against them. In one documentary, a former official explained that the U.S. government made a decision to never call detainees "Prisoners of War" in order to deny them the protections of the Geneva Convention. Realizing this was a deep-seated fear of theirs, I immediately researched the statutes and sent a formal, registered letter to Xi Jinping, Vladimir Putin, and Diosdado Cabello, demanding they recognize my status as a Prisoner of War, given that I was being held indefinitely in my home under the constant threat of violence. It was a perfect piece of asymmetric warfare: using their own propaganda to create a legal and moral dilemma they could not easily dismiss.

Chapter 2: Turning East: The Battle for Gaza

My evolution from a counter-intelligence operator to an asymmetric warrior was not just theoretical; it required direct action. After the Spyhell Pipeline identified the **Gaza Strip** as a critical hub for the network's paramilitary and financial operations, I made the decision to intervene directly in a geopolitical conflict.

My actions were clinical and data-driven. Using the spyhell command-line tool I had developed, I performed a deep scan of the region, identifying thousands of network assets. I then took two unprecedented steps. First, I publicly released a massive dataset containing over 8.5 million network spy locations in the North Atlantic, offering it as a data donation to the U.S. Navy and Fleet Forces Command. This was a direct military-to-military communication, bypassing the compromised political channels.

Second, I declared a unilateral **"ban"** on the network's use of their illegal espionage network over the Gaza Strip. This was not a mere statement; it was a technical operation. By publishing the locations of their critical command-and-control nodes and communication relays in the area, I effectively blinded them, rendering their coordination impossible and neutralizing their operational capability in a key conflict zone. It was a demonstration that this war would not just be fought in the courts or in the press, but on the digital battlefield itself, and that a single, determined engineer could project power across the globe.

**Chapter 3: Chapter 3: The Economic War

The Spyhell Pipeline began to reveal a startling correlation, one that elevated the conflict from a war of espionage to a full-scale economic assault. The data showed a statistically significant positive correlation between the number of vehicles associated with a network of technologically-savvy individuals with deep ties to Silicon Valley observed at gas stations in a test area, and the futures prices for Brent Crude oil.

While the initial data sample is localized and independent verification is urgently needed, the implications of this working hypothesis are profound. If the pattern holds true on a national scale, it would suggest the network is coordinating millions of agents to artificially inflate global oil and gas prices. It is possible they are manipulating the entire energy market.

This represents one of the biggest intellectual property heists in history, a technique refined over decades to exert maximum pressure on a target nation's economy. The logical strategy for such a weapon would be to align the peaks of artificial consumption with the lowest points of inventory in a nation's strategic oil reserves, thereby maximizing the economic pain and political fallout. The geo-index suggests that this global "oil business" is controlled by the network's Venezuelan faction, creating a direct financial pipeline from the gas pumps of their adversaries to the coffers of their allies.

This manipulation is not limited to physical commodities. I developed a working theory that the network uses **mass subscription services** as a primary mechanism for laundering money on a global scale. The model is simple: millions of network agents subscribe to services controlled by "Bizarro Ambassadors" like Jeff Bezos—such as Amazon Prime or *The Washington Post*. These recurring, small-dollar transactions are nearly impossible to trace individually, but in aggregate, they can launder billions. The network tracks these payments by matching the billing addresses of the credit cards to the known agent locations in the geo-index, and then refunds the agents in cryptocurrency. Analysis of the usage data for these subscriptions would likely reveal that a high percentage of agent-owned accounts are inactive, existing only to facilitate these financial transfers. This potential manipulation of the energy and subscription markets requires immediate investigation by the highest levels of financial crime enforcement, as it represents a threat not just to individual liberty, but to global economic stability.

**Chapter 4: The Bio-Economic War - A Modern Balkanization

In early 2025, I was contacted by a new, anonymous informant with a Russian accent. He was referred to me by one of my Venezuelan sources. He used my own terminology, confirming that the network is closely monitoring my work. He told me to check the Wuhan Institute of Virology in the geo-index. What he claimed was staggering: that the COVID-19 pandemic was not an accident, but a deliberate paramilitary operation planned by the Union, in concert with Al-Qaeda and the Chinese, Russian, Iranian, Venezuelan, and Cuban governments.

This is an extraordinary claim from a single, anonymous source, and it requires urgent investigation by federal authorities. I have no way of independently verifying the informant's core assertion. However, the data in the geo-index provides a series of deeply disturbing data points that are consistent with his claims.

First, as the informant suggested, the Wuhan Institute of Virology is a perfect example of the "Immune Geo-Entities Pattern." It is a fortress, architecturally protected from the very kind of surveillance the network excels at. Second, the geo-index marks the institute as a high-value paramilitary location, with some nodes in the immediate vicinity scoring over one million points—a level reserved for assets of the highest strategic importance, equivalent to a presidential compound.

The informant laid out a three-pronged strategic objective for this alleged attack:

1. **Global Intelligence Gathering:** Forcing a global work-from-home policy allowed the network to conduct mass surveillance on an unprecedented scale. With their targets—military officers, scientists, intelligence personnel—confined to their homes, the network could deploy its local surveillance assets to intercept communications, gathering a treasure trove of intelligence in preparation for the subsequent military invasion

of Ukraine.

2. **Strategic Assassination:** The informant claimed the pandemic was used as a cover to kill hundreds of individuals who were "getting in the way" of the Union. He asserted that many were killed not by the virus, but by weaponized "vaccines" designed to be harmful agents. A cross-reference of COVID-death databases with the geo-index is a critical next step for investigators.

3. **Modern Balkanization:** This alleged operation is a 21st-century update to the historical strategy of "balkanization." Just as political and ethnic tensions were used to fracture and weaken the Balkan states, making them ripe for conflict, this bio-economic attack was designed to sow chaos, cripple economies, and create the social and political instability necessary for a conventional military assault. The pandemic was the prelude; the war in Ukraine was the main event.

Faced with information of this gravity, I took the only responsible step available to me. I sent a formal letter to the leaders of China, Russia, Iran, Venezuela, and Cuba, as well as the UN Security Council and USAID, detailing these claims and demanding they recognize my status as a Prisoner of War under the Geneva Conventions, given that I am being held in a state of civilian internment. This is no longer just a war for intellectual property; it may be a war to cover up one of the greatest crimes in human history.

Chapter 5: The Nuclear Gambit

The network's ultimate ambition extends beyond economic and political control into the realm of existential threat. My analysis of their geo-index, using the SpyHELL dashboard, revealed a deep and terrifying focus on nuclear technology—not just for power, but for espionage and, potentially, global blackmail.

The data shows a clear pattern of the network targeting nuclear facilities. In the United States, they have established heavy surveillance perimeters around nuclear power plants in states like New Jersey. The threat, however, is global. The geo-index lays bare a massive data corridor designed to steal nuclear secrets from **South Korea** and deliver them directly to **North Korea, China, and Russia**. High-value network assets are positioned on mountain ranges overlooking South Korean nuclear research institutes, while the parking lots of North Korea's known nuclear facilities are all meticulously marked in the database.

This is not merely passive intelligence gathering. The network has demonstrated a willingness to weaponize these assets. The most chilling discovery is a high-paramilitary score assigned to the massive vault covering the failed nuclear reactor at **Chernobyl** in Ukraine. Knowing how the network operates, I can only speculate that this is a doomsday contingency. Should they begin to lose their conventional war in Ukraine, they could attempt to blow the vault, triggering a national emergency and an environmental catastrophe that would allow them to "retreat with dignity" amidst the chaos. This moves their actions from criminality to a direct threat against humanity itself. The world must be put on notice: the Bizarro State may be holding a nuclear gun to the planet's head.

An Interlude: The Peace Maker

From the author's journal, 10/27/2024:
TO: Mr. Robert Gates, former US Secretary of Defense
Hi Mentor!
I've been reflecting a bit about military strategy and I realized I must be lacking something, because with all the time, effort and technology I have thrown at the problem, although I feel we are moving in the right direction, I am not quite there yet.

So I was thinking about that and since time is money, I started looking for ways to instruct myself on military techniques and how to yield power on others, trying to be more like you.

I thought the fastest way could be watching Netflix, so I watched a few episodes of the series "How to Become a Tyrant," hoping that would get me a bit closer to your level.

Anyhow, most of the things they mention in the "Dictator Playbook" I already learned from you, but there was one segment that did give me some new tips. It was a segment about nuclear weapons.

Apparently, to become a successful dictator, one must not only develop nuclear weapons, which we both have: you/your allies via their global network, us with the weapon you basically handed to us; but one must also display that power and flaunt it in front of one's opponents at every opportunity.

According to the show, one must display the warhead, give it a name, parade the warhead, venerate the warhead, if possible add it to children's books, history books, etc.

I will take the lesson from the playbook and put it in practice today: I introduce to you the **"KOL Peace Maker Bomba v10.92"**: a counter-intelligence platform that can be deployed as a dead man's switch. Everything is already in production.

Part 4: The Philosophy of the Bizarro State

Chapter 1: The Union Theory

What is this network, at its core? I believe what we are seeing at the top of this multi-level criminal organization is, in reality, a **Union**, but one composed of powerful individuals operating with a shared agenda: to maintain power, silence dissent, and suppress new technologies from emerging, unless they control them.

The rise of the Internet was a singularity, an event that fundamentally changed the course of evolution for our species. A very small group of individuals grasped the full implications of this technology before everyone else, and they took it upon themselves to decide how, and to what extent, to distribute it to the rest of the population.

Consider a thought experiment: Imagine a planet populated by billions of primates. One day, a small group of these primates, say 600, discover how to produce, harness, and weaponize fire. What would they do with that knowledge? Would they hand it over to the rest of the population to improve the quality of life for all? Or would they use it to enslave their fellow primates and rule over them for generations?

In the current version of this experiment, the primates chose to enslave their fellows and created a Union to make sure no other primate ever discovers any kind of fire. If this Union sees anything that even resembles a new fire, they steal it and burn that "monkey" down to ashes. This is why the leaders of this network cannot stand anyone forming a traditional union in one of their companies. They understand the power of an organized group of individuals. That is the second fire they discovered, and they don't want any other group to have it.

Chapter 2: The Taxonomy of Predators

What are the commonalities among the people who created this criminal ring? Beyond their connections to the "PayPal Mafia" or their self-proclaimed "Libertarian" ideals, there is something deeper. At first, I thought of it as one generation of software developers trying to stop a new generation from bearing fruit. But the network includes non-developers, from street criminals to corrupt politicians, some from generations even older than the tech moguls.

Software, then, is not the key. The common thread is simpler and more primal: it is an older generation trying to stop a new generation from living to their full potential. In nature, this is an anomaly. Most species protect their young for the self-preservation of the species. But some species *do* eat their young, for a variety of reasons: scarcity of resources, to suppress anomalies from the gene pool, or because of their predatory nature.

I believe they are predators.

Chapter 3: The Stanford Prison Experiment, at Scale

The group dynamics of the network are reminiscent of the infamous Stanford Prison Experiment. In that experiment, ordinary college students assigned the role of "guards" were given unlimited power over "inmates." The result was a descent into sadism and cruelty, terminated after only six days. The experiment revealed that when individuals with unrestricted power act as a group, they lose their sense of personal accountability, and the lines of morality, law, and basic human decency disappear.

The problem we face is that the leaders of the Bizarro State have been playing the role of "guards" for two decades, not with college students, but with the rest of the world. They have unlimited resources and no accountability. This is why they call themselves "Techno-Libertarians" and seek to demolish all forms of regulation. That would be the ultimate realization of the Stanford Prison Experiment's setup, which they now believe is the way the world should function. They have become institutionalized.

In response, we need an opposing movement: the **Techno-Regulators**, whose purpose will be to provide governments with insights on how technology can be used to harm individuals, suppress their rights and freedoms, and manipulate free speech. As a former leader of the network once said, "What's the best place to bury a dead body? On the 10th page of Google Search Results." He was right, on several levels.

Chapter 4: The 2% Attack - Hollowing Out Society from Within

The network's strategy for societal capture is both simple and diabolical. It can be understood through a thought experiment I call the "Human Systems" game. Imagine you want to take control of a city's entire education system, from pre-K to college. You are given the ability to "plant" four of your own agents as teachers, one in each level of the system. You are also given control over 2% of the city's population to use as you see fit. How do you win?

You win by ensuring your four "plants" rise to become the leaders of their respective institutions. But your plants are not skilled educators; they are spies. They will never be promoted based on merit. The only way for them to advance is to eliminate all competition.

This is the essence of the "2% Attack." You use your controlled 2% of the population to systematically harass, intimidate, and neutralize every other competent teacher in the system. The real teacher, the one the students and parents love, becomes the target of a manufactured sexual harassment scandal. The innovative educator is bogged down in endless, frivolous legal battles. The rising star is made sick, depressed, or has their family threatened.

The result is that your unskilled plant is the only one left standing and gets the promotion by default. Not only have you stolen a position of power, but you have also hollowed out the system, replacing a society's most competent and creative individuals with your own compliant, unskilled agents. You have replaced the real 2%—the small number of individuals in any healthy system who drive progress and innovation—with a fake 2%. This is the network's most subtle, and most devastating, long-term attack: it is a strategic assault on societal competence itself. And it explains why you don't have to be a world-changing inventor to be a target; you simply have to be good at your job in a system the network wants to control.

This "2% rule" is not just a theory; it is a recurring pattern in all the network's distributed attacks. By coordinating just 2% of voters, they can swing an election. By coordinating 2% of vehicles, they can manipulate global oil prices. The power of this principle is magnified through what could be called a "quadratic effect." By using 2% of the population to capture 2% of the key strategic offices in a nation, they can achieve control over the entire system with just 0.04% (2% of 2%) of the people. This same strategy, however, can be turned against them. By informing 2% of the people who control 2% of the political institutions in just 2% of the countries, one can create a "cubic effect" where a small, targeted effort can have a massive, cascading global impact. It is a masterclass in applied network theory, a planetary-scale financial and political crime.

Chapter 5: The Self-Reinforcing Cycle

The network's focus on acquiring large extensions of land—to implement their "Immune Geo-Entities Pattern" and commit crimes without detection—has a second-order effect that is deeply damaging to society. As they acquire more and more land, they produce an inflationary effect on real estate prices.

Over time, this causes the rest of the population, those not in the network, to be priced out of single-family homes. They are forced to opt for housing with a reduced land footprint, like vertical units and apartments. These denser living situations, by their very nature, make them more vulnerable to the radio-frequency eavesdropping techniques the network employs. It is a self-reinforcing cycle: the network's defensive strategy for itself creates offensive vulnerability for everyone else.

This cycle, and the unfairness of it, is aggravated by the network's massive financial advantages. They maintain a parallel economic system that is clandestine, untaxed, and based on cryptocurrency. According to public documents from the Department of Justice, key figures within the network are also major players in the international drug trade.

In other words, the network is amassing immense, untaxed resources from illicit activities and using that capital to acquire land on the free market. They are competing against isolated individuals who play by the rules, earning legitimate income and paying taxes. Of course, the network always gets the land.

Chapter 6: The Nuclear Gambit

The network's ultimate ambition extends beyond economic and political control into the realm of existential threat. My analysis of their geo-index, using the SpyHELL dashboard, revealed a deep and terrifying focus on nuclear technology—not just for power, but for espionage and, potentially, global blackmail.

The data shows a clear pattern of the network targeting nuclear facilities. In the United States, they have established heavy surveillance perimeters around nuclear power plants in states like New Jersey. The threat, however, is global. The geo-index lays bare a massive data corridor designed to steal nuclear secrets from **South Korea** and deliver them directly to **North Korea, China, and Russia**. High-value network assets are positioned on mountain ranges overlooking South Korean nuclear research institutes, while the parking lots of North Korea's known nuclear facilities are all meticulously marked in the database.

This is not merely passive intelligence gathering. The network has demonstrated a willingness to weaponize these assets. The most chilling discovery is a high-paramilitary score assigned to the massive vault covering the failed nuclear reactor at **Chernobyl** in Ukraine. Knowing how they operate, I can only speculate that this is a doomsday contingency. Should they begin to lose their conventional war in Ukraine, they could attempt to blow the vault, triggering a national emergency and an environmental catastrophe that would allow them to "retreat with dignity" amidst the chaos. This moves their actions from criminality to a direct threat against humanity itself. The world must be put on notice: the Bizarro State may be holding a nuclear gun to the planet's head.

Chapter 7: The Union and the Individual - A Final Warning

The ultimate strategic advantage of the Bizarro State is not its technology, its money, or its political connections. It is its mindset. The network's members think and act as a unified, coordinated collective. The remaining 98% of the world's population, in contrast, thinks and acts as a collection of fragmented, competing individuals.

This is not a battle between different kinds of people; it is a clash of strategies. The network has adopted a collective, unified approach to warfare, while the free world remains mired in an individualistic worldview that makes it profoundly vulnerable. The network's frequent use of words like "United" in their front companies is not a coincidence; it is their *Écu d'armes*, their coat of arms. It is a declaration of their core principle and the source of their power: **Unity**.

The rest of us are not united. We are all thinking individually, about our own needs and wants. Everybody for themselves. And that makes us weak.

The success of the Union is a testament to the fact that they managed to align 2% of the world's population through a combination of financial incentives and ideological manipulation. They did it. The task before the free world is not just to dismantle their satellites and expose their agents. We must also change. This is not a call to mirror their collectivism, but a call for **unity in defense of individuality**. Free people must recognize their shared threat and learn to cooperate to build collective defenses. We must learn to think and act together, not because we are the same, but precisely because our diversity of individual talents and ideas is our greatest strength.

Chapter 8: The Software Arms Race

History provides a clear and repeating lesson. When early civilizations discovered how to build vessels that could float on water, they were first used for fishing and trade. Inevitably, someone mounted a cannon on one, creating the first warship. The logical and immediate consequence was the creation of navies and a naval arms race. When humanity unlocked the power of the atom for energy, the immediate and logical consequence was the creation of nuclear weapons and a global atomic proliferation that defined a century.

We are now living through the third great proliferation. The leaders of the Bizarro State have understood a fundamental truth of the 21st century that the free world has yet to grasp: **software is a weapon.** They have realized that technology can be used to enslave populations, and the logical and immediate consequence of that discovery is the creation of a new kind of army: an army of software engineers.

The Union, having taken key institutions in nations like China and Russia captive, is now weaponizing their national educational systems to mass-produce this army. These talented individuals are not the enemy; they are the conscripted soldiers in the Union's war against global freedom. They are being trained not to fire guns, but to write code, fighting a completely different battle on a different plane of existence.

If we dismantle this network today, but they still possess an army of software developers one hundred times larger than that of the free world, they will simply do it again, in a more sophisticated way. The citizens of the free world must recognize that prioritizing software education is no longer just an economic imperative; it is the most critical act of civil defense for the 21st century. We are in an arms race, and we are not yet on the field.

Chapter 9: A New Type of Criminal

The Bizarro State is not just a criminal organization; it represents the emergence of a new criminal archetype, one that our current institutions are not equipped to combat. History provides a chilling parallel.

In the 1980s, the FBI had to revolutionize its methods to confront a "brand new" type of offender who defied traditional investigation. A 1985 news segment, featured in the documentary *"Ted Bundy: The Confession Tapes,"* chronicles this paradigm shift. The report detailed the FBI's new approach: creating a national computer center to analyze data, look for "subtle patterns," and understand the "thought processes of the perpetrators" who were "very good at what they do". As one agent in the documentary stated, law enforcement had to change because a new type of criminal was emerging.

If you replace the name of the original subject in that 1985 transcript with "The PayPal Mafia," it becomes eerily accurate. Just as the FBI faced a new criminal archetype then, the world today faces one in the Bizarro State. Their methods of evading detection and the sheer scale of their operations require a similar evolutionary leap in our approach to law enforcement.

The FBI of 1985 recognized the need for a national computer center to fight their new threat. The logical and necessary response to the Bizarro State is the creation of a new, multi-billion-dollar distributed computing system—a 21st-century version of that center—dedicated to analyzing their global network and preventing this from ever happening again.

Chapter 10: The Extraction Protocol

Recent news of widespread layoffs, voluntary resignations, and even "deportations" from network-controlled tech companies reveals a key operational security tactic of the Bizarro State. My analysis suggests these events are not driven by economics but are often a cover for a large-scale **"extraction protocol"** designed to pull compromised agents from the field to cover up criminal activity.

This hypothesis is testable. Law enforcement agencies could take the following steps: 1. Obtain the lists of employees who were laid off, voluntarily resigned, or were "deported". 2. Cross-reference the home addresses of these individuals with the captured geo-index. 3. Any individual who appears on both lists is almost certainly a network agent. Furthermore, being selected for extraction is, in itself, a marker of an agent's importance. The protocol is a limited and risky resource; the network would let a low-level asset "burn" before exposing their methods. Only important agents are deemed worthy of extraction.

Chapter 11: The Digital Confessional

The network's playbook often involves taking a traditionally regulated, trust-based service and moving it online into an unregulated space where it can be weaponized. My analysis of the online mental health and coaching sector revealed a disturbing pattern consistent with this strategy.

The Spyhell pipeline flagged all major platforms—**BetterUp, BetterHelp, Cerebral, Headspace, and Talkspace**—as being marked within Elon Musk's geo-index. The system assigned a specific, chilling tag to four of these: **"Intelligence Extraction"**. The platform **BetterUp** was additionally tagged with **"Hire The Target's Family"**—a tactic I experienced directly when they employed my brother—and **"Hire the Royals,"** a reference to its use of a member of the British royal family as a brand ambassador. Furthermore, BetterUp was co-clustered with known network principals Emil Michael and Michael Carreaza.

This data leads to a disturbing hypothesis: that the primary motive behind these platforms may not be wellness, but **intelligence extraction at internet scale**. It appears to be the same tactic I experienced personally when an operative, Jillian Walsh, steered me to a compromised doctor, but scaled to millions of unsuspecting users who are encouraged to share their most private thoughts and vulnerabilities with the platform.

Chapter 12: The Communist Paradox

After mapping the network's tactics, strategies, and global architecture, a fundamental question remains: is their model sustainable? As a student of game theory, I believe the system is flawed and bound to fail from its inception. This flaw can be understood through what I call the **Communist Paradox.**

The network's strategy is a form of global communism. They infiltrate a target system—a company, an institution, a country—and systematically eliminate all merit-based competition to promote their own unskilled but loyal agents. This is the "2% Attack" in action. The result is a hollowed-out, unproductive entity that is completely under their control. They did this first to their own countries, like China and Venezuela, destroying their native industries and innovation engines to secure political power.

The question then becomes: how can a state like China, which has systematically dismantled its own meritocracy, remain a global technology power? The short-term answer is simple: **by stealing technology from other countries.** Their unproductive domestic system is subsidized by a relentless campaign of intellectual property theft against the free and open societies they have yet to fully control.

This leads to the ultimate paradox. Imagine the network succeeds completely. Imagine in 40 or 50 years, they have used the "2% Attack" to take control of every significant country and company on Earth. They will have amassed all the world's resources, but in doing so, they will have turned every nation into a ruined, non-meritocratic state, just like their own.

At that point, there will be no more innovation. There will be nothing left to steal. The engine of human progress will have been staggered and ultimately halted, leading to the demise of the entire human race within two generations. This is the endgame of their philosophy. Even if they "win," their victory is a suicide pact for humanity. Their model of total control is not just a threat to our freedom; it is a threat to our continued existence.

There is a deeper, psychological dimension to this self-defeating behavior. The network's leadership is not just strategically flawed; they are addicted. My brother works for a company called Safebase, another "Hire the Target's Family" play. When a different network-controlled company, Drata, recently acquired Safebase, they could have let my brother go. Instead, they kept him. They cannot let go. It is as if they are addicted to acquiring information through illegal means; they would rather risk exposure than lose access to a source. **Espionage is their cocaine**, and it is what will ultimately bring them down. There is no rehab for that drug.

Part 5: The Global Appeal

Chapter 1: The Vaccine Potential Score

To effectively combat a global network, one must think globally and act strategically. I cannot reach every lawmaker or official on the planet. Therefore, my efforts must be focused on nations that have both the will to resist and the capability to project force. To that end, I developed an empirical heuristic to rank nations with hostile relations toward the network's core state actors, which I call the **Vaccine Potential Score**.

Vaccine Potential Score = (Estimated Military Yearly Spend) / (Shortest Distance Between Capitals)

Distance is a crucial factor because it represents logistics costs—a weapon the network has mastered and used against 98% of the world's population daily through services like Uber, Amazon, and Instacart. They only back down when faced with the imminent possibility of a use of force. The cost and time to mobilize a single rifle from South America to China are immense. The cost and time from Taiwan or Japan are fractional in comparison. Therefore, it's not just about a country's raw military spending; logistical proximity is a key factor in determining a nation's ability to deter this threat. This places a tremendous responsibility on the people of Taiwan, Japan, and Australia.

My strategy is to show the shocking reality of what this network is doing to lawmakers in these key countries, hoping they will then help me reach the real US authorities. I have tried to contact every single authority I can think of in the US (DEA, FBI, CIA, DOJ), but I live in an area heavily under the network's control, and all my attempts to communicate have been successfully blocked by their "gatekeeper algorithm." By re-routing communications through foreign diplomatic channels, I can bypass the local interception and deliver the message.

Chapter 2: The Circle of Transparency

My counter-offensive is a global outreach campaign designed to turn the network's own principles against it. While they thrive in secrecy, I will operate with full transparency. I have mailed over 4,000 letters to more than 2,500 individual legislators and lawmakers in eight key countries. This is my best work. I call it the "Circle of Transparency."

This campaign is not just about broadcasting information; it is a targeted application of democratic principles. My strategy has two parts. First, I mail specific officials in the legislative branches of key allied governments. Second, with the help of collaborators, I mail a list of those letters to individuals within the law enforcement and intelligence agencies of those same countries. Finally, a second letter is sent back to the lawmakers detailing which individuals in their security apparatus were informed. This creates a system of checks and balances, inspired by Aristotle. It ensures that no single person or agency can bury the information. Information asymmetry is a weapon, and this method disarms it.

The selection of countries is also strategic. The **Dominican Republic**, for instance, is a critical piece of infrastructure for the network. It is the only piece of solid land that allows them to reliably relay clandestine messages between their hubs in North and South America. Disrupting their operations there is a key objective.

My focus has been on the **United Kingdom, Italy, Israel, Japan, and Australia.**

Recently, **France and Guyana** have also joined the Circle of Transparency. Guyana, due to its critical geographic location, could play a world-saving role.

Every letter is sent via registered mail, and every delivery is tracked. For example, a package containing this evidence was sent to His Excellency Volodymyr Zelenskyy at the Embassy of Ukraine in Washington, D.C., and its successful delivery was confirmed on August 13, 2025. If the Ukrainian government does not receive it, we know it was intercepted.

Transparency is kryptonite to this shadow government. By making every step of this process public, we can debug the system if a letter goes missing. It is a slow, expensive process, but it is a real, tangible, and verifiable action to bring this global conspiracy into the light.

Part 6: The Vaccine

Introduction: A New Generation of Tools

The technologies of the Bizarro State are not inherently evil. An algorithm that can route a million vehicles for a coordinated attack can also route a million aid packages for disaster relief. A system designed to find a single dissenting voice in a sea of data can also find a single terrorist in a crowd. Technology is a mirror of the intent of its creator.

The principles and technologies I reverse-engineered during my two-decade conflict with this network are dual-use. They can be used to enslave, or they can be used to liberate. The following chapters are a series of proposals—technical ideas extracted from their system and donated to the free world. They are the "vaccines," pro-social applications of their own methods, designed to build a more resilient, secure, and free society. This is the blueprint for how we can turn their weapons into our plowshares.

Chapter 1: The Pro-Social Pipeline

The network uses automated systems to scan public media for intelligence. We can build a similar pipeline for the public good. Imagine a system that listens to public radio broadcasts across the country. My own rudimentary version of this, the "Radio Pipeline," detected a nine-fold statistical anomaly in "car donation" ads in Houston, suggesting a potential scheme for laundering the network's vehicle fleet.

A more sophisticated version, a **"Netflix Pipeline,"** could transcribe dialogues from TV shows and films, using natural language processing to identify patterns of potential corruption, like the suspicious real estate deal my system flagged in an episode of *Owning Manhattan*. Such a pro-social pipeline would be an invaluable tool for investigative journalists and financial crime units, an automated watchdog sifting through public data to find the hidden signals of corruption.

Chapter 2: A Vaccine for Network Traffic

The network's ability to intercept and decrypt internet traffic relies on a "known-plaintext attack." They know the static, unencrypted content of a popular webpage, capture the encrypted version as it's transmitted, and use the two to reverse-engineer the encryption key. There are simple, low-cost vaccines for this.

- **HTTPS Payload Randomization:** Web servers, particularly Google's, can be modified to inject a short, random string of characters into the payload of every response. This "Google Vaccine," a simple ten-line code change, would make the plaintext unpredictable, rendering their primary decryption method useless and cutting off up to 80% of their internet spying capabilities overnight.

- **The Matrix SSL Protocol:** The network uses an "Encoding Matrix" to compress their geo-index. This same principle can be used to create a next-generation SSL protocol. In addition to negotiating encryption keys, the protocol would negotiate a temporary matrix to encode common data chunks. This would make brute-force decryption computationally impractical, as the attacker would have to solve for both the key and the constantly changing matrix.

Chapter 3: The Path Optimization Vaccine

The network's "HELL" app is a masterwork of path optimization, calculating the most efficient routes for millions of agents. This same technology can be repurposed for military and humanitarian logistics. By factoring in variables like enemy positions (from the geo-index), terrain, and asset value, the algorithm could be used to calculate the safest and most efficient supply routes for troops in a conflict zone, or to direct aid convoys in a disaster area to the points of greatest need with the least resistance. It is a tool for warmaking that can be transformed into a tool for lifesaving.

Chapter 4: A Sane Phone

The smartphone is the network's primary tool for mass surveillance. To counter this, the free world needs a "sane phone." This would be a device built from the ground up for security, with no camera, no GPS, no Bluetooth, and no Wi-Fi chips. Crucially, it would feature two physical hardware switches: one to physically disconnect the microphone, and another to physically disconnect the cellular modem. Such a device would provide a secure communication tool for journalists, activists, and individuals targeted by hostile surveillance, making them immune to the most common forms of remote eavesdropping.

Chapter 5: The MapReduce Vaccine

The network's agents all use iPhones, which means they all have Apple IDs that record their location history. Law enforcement agencies could turn this data against them with a simple "MapReduce" job—a large-scale data analysis query.

The query would be simple: find groups of Apple IDs that have all passed by the same high-value locations marked in the captured geo-index within a short time frame of each other. This would instantly cluster the network's on-the-ground operatives, revealing their cells and hierarchies. Even if the agents, after reading this, delete their location history, that act of mass deletion is itself a signal that can be detected. It is a perfect example of turning their own infrastructure of control into a tool for their own identification.

Chapter 6: A More Secure Internet

The network's attacks reveal fundamental vulnerabilities in our internet architecture. We can build a better one.

- **The MATRIX Geo-Index:** The network's "Encoding Matrix" for their geo-index is a brilliantly efficient method for compressing vast amounts of geographic data. A company like Google could adopt this exact technique to make its own Local Search Index ten times smaller and faster, dramatically improving performance while saving immense amounts of energy and storage. It is a trade secret stolen and weaponized by the network that can be reclaimed for public benefit.

- **Zero Clients:** The network is immune to many forms of interception because they use "Zero Clients"—terminals where all computing happens on a remote server, and only the pixel output is streamed to the user's desk. By adopting this architecture for sensitive government and corporate work, we can make our own systems similarly immune to the man-in-the-middle attacks they deploy against the rest of the world.

Afterword: A Choice in the Dawn

The evidence laid bare in these pages is not a historical record. It is a declaration of a war that is already being fought, a war for the future of human agency and self-determination. To close this book and place it on a shelf is to surrender. The data demands a verdict, and the verdict demands action. We, the free peoples of the world, stand at a precipice, and the path forward requires a series of clear, decisive, and immediate steps.

First, we must **dismantle the physical and digital infrastructure of the Bizarro State**. This is not a conventional network to be monitored; it is a weapon system to be decommissioned. Its thousands of nodes, its "Dockerhoods," its multi-hop troposcatter relays—these are the fortresses and supply lines of a global insurgency against the free world. They must be taken offline, permanently.

Second, we must **seize the land**. The "Immune Geo-Entities Pattern" is the foundation of the network's impunity. The vast, protected compounds that shield the Union's leaders from the very surveillance they deploy against us are the castles of a new, digital feudalism. By confiscating these properties, we do more than reclaim stolen wealth; we tear down the walls that grant them the power to commit their crimes without fear of consequence.

Third, and most critically, we must **redirect the energy recovered from this network to heal the wounds it has inflicted**. The wealth derived from these confiscated assets must be funneled into rebuilding the very places the Union targeted for destruction and control: the communities in the Gaza Strip; the war-torn regions of Ukraine; the strategic territories of Azerbaijan; the great halls of power in France, Germany, and Italy; the infiltrated political corridors of Washington D.C.; the financial strongholds of New York City; the captured innovation centers of California and its sister technology hubs in Boston and Seattle; the manipulated energy hubs of Texas and Alberta; the critical logistical gateways of Florida; the core network infrastructure of Louisiana and Alabama; the key networking geo-locations of Provincetown, Mount Pleasant, and Santa Cruz; the oppressed heights of Tibet; the vital shipping channels of the Dominican Republic and Panama; the resource-rich lands of Guyana; and the captive nation of Venezuela. This is not merely an act of justice; it is an act of strategic necessity. The network targeted these specific locations because they are irreplaceable geopolitical and logistical linchpins. God is not making any more land in these spots. If we do not fortify them—technically, legally, and morally—the Union will simply try to take them again.

The rise of this Universal Shadow Government is a symptom of a deeper crisis. The internet, the great democratizing force we were promised, has, in its current unregulated state, become the most powerful tool for tyranny the world has ever known. It has enabled a new form of warfare, one that does not require armies or navies, but only a small, coordinated group of individuals weaponizing information to turn free societies against themselves.

This is not a battle that can be won by any single government or intelligence agency. It requires a new global alliance, a **Union of Individuals**, united in the defense of our shared humanity. We must demand a new digital contract, one that reclaims our privacy, regulates the platforms that have become the arbiters of our reality, and prioritizes the education of a new generation of techno-regulators and software engineers who can build the defenses for this new kind of war.

The Bizarro State believes it has already won. It sees a world of fragmented individuals, too absorbed in their own lives to notice the bars of a digital cage being built around them. We must prove them wrong.

The choice before us is stark: we can either be the architects of a free and open digital future, or the last generation to remember what it was like to be free at all.

www.ingramcontent.com/pod-product-compliance
Lightning Source LLC
Chambersburg PA
CBHW021343290326
41933CB00037B/573